WORD OF DOG

....

MEGAN ANDERSON

FREMANTLE PRESS

For all the thinking dogs

Introduction

In more than two decades as a journalist, I've learned a couple of things about how to get the best from an interview: pose good questions, then shut up and listen.

Once they're on a roll, people can be refreshingly candid about life and how they feel about it. They'll reveal their quirks and foibles, the worries that keep them up at night, their deepest passions, the choices they regret, the hopes they hold onto, the most embarrassing things in their fridge. When it's authentic and unscripted, it's gold.

The journalistic style in this book is an homage to the fading art of listening and the power of the direct quote. Everyone has something to say. Sometimes it's deep, often it's trivial, occasionally it's awkward. The snatches of dialogue in the book are mostly celebrations of the ordinary: an unsanitised take on what it is to be alive.

I owe thanks to the unsuspecting friends (and a few eavesdropped-upon strangers) from whom I filched one-liners or seeds of ideas for this work. I'd never have dreamed up a bottle of red and a basket of ironing on my own. Probably not patchouli-phobic shop assistants, either.

And why dogs? When I was making a career shift into art land, they struck me as a great choice to bring along for the ride: layered enough to be stimulating company, genuine enough to keep things real, and playful enough to make this not feel like work at all.

They're certainly too transparent to fake a nonchalant pose, so they're seldom seen sitting nicely in my artwork. More often they're captured mid-apology, or mid-question, or shooting a withering glance sideways, or tripping over their ears — whatever is happening for them in the moment. They're all about the truth.

In this book, dogs play the part of whimsical, disarming, slightly absurd bearers of the human condition. They really are the best people.

" I took up Uber driving when I lost my job on the mine. I used to drive a Cat 793F haul truck, with wheels the size of houses. I drive a second-hand Pulsar now. I work at night mostly, so my passengers are well lubricated a lot of the time. They can be entertaining, but just as often they pass out in the back. When that happens I sometimes take a detour around the river to gawp at the penthouses and watch the lights twinkling. I crank up the classical music and pretend I'm a Russian oligarch in an Aston Martin DB5. The night sky really excites my imagination. "

" I used to get my gear off at the back beaches a bit. I really
got a taste for it in the summer of '09 when I was in peak
shape and had discovered spray tans. I'm a fully-fledged
nudist now. The core crew from the beach formed an
incorporated body to give the whole thing some legitimacy,
and we do a lot of activities together. Lawn bowls is one of
my favourites: it's so nice to feel the soft grass under your
feet. We sit around wearing smiles and nothing else — except
sunscreen, obviously. It's really liberating. There's a bit of
etiquette around where to plant your eyes, but nobody is
very uptight about it. I'm not ripped anymore, but I don't care
because it's not about posing anyway. It's about letting go of
all your caked-on anxieties and inhibitions. I've had some of
the most real and refreshing conversations of my life while
in the nuddy. I've also learned a lot about finances —
I'm the treasurer. "

BRUCE

RESTING HEART RATE:	88 bpm
FOND OF:	Belting out a bit of Farnsey in the shower
BOTHERED BY:	Close talkers
ONE GREAT WORD:	Squeegee
SPARKLING OR STILL:	Tap water is fine

"Some say everything happens for a reason, but I think everything happens for no reason at all. Life is a series of random collisions of atoms and opinions and cyclists and coffee and chance meetings and close calls and break-ups and black cats and stray feathers and great pizza and disappointing handshakes, among other things. None of it has anything to do with anything. That's my world view."

66 We met on a blue moon. Not just a blue moon — it was a super moon, and a blood moon as well. What are the chances? We were at the same interstate conference and we'd both skipped the delegates' dinner to walk solo on the beach under that dramatic sky. I recognised her upright gait from the breakfast buffet. She recognised me because I'd forgotten to take off my stupid lanyard. We got chatting in the moonlight and I liked her right away. You know why? She didn't ask me what I thought of the keynote speaker. She didn't even mention stem cells. She just asked me what kind of teapot I have at home, and that's when I knew. We've been together seven years now. I'm not itchy. I don't think she's itchy either. My teapot is glass, by the way. I like hibiscus loose leaf. She's more of an Earl Grey girl. 99

66 I'm not lost.
I'm exploring my boundaries. **99**

13

You've got to put love in your food. When you make a sandwich, spread the chutney right to the edges. Don't slap your ingredients down; take your time. Handle your ham like it's lace. Give your tomato a tender squeeze. Wash your lettuce one leaf at a time. Pat it dry with paper towel — the expensive stuff. This is not just a sandwich. It's an expression of hope and kindness. If more of us put love into our food, maybe we could have peace on earth.

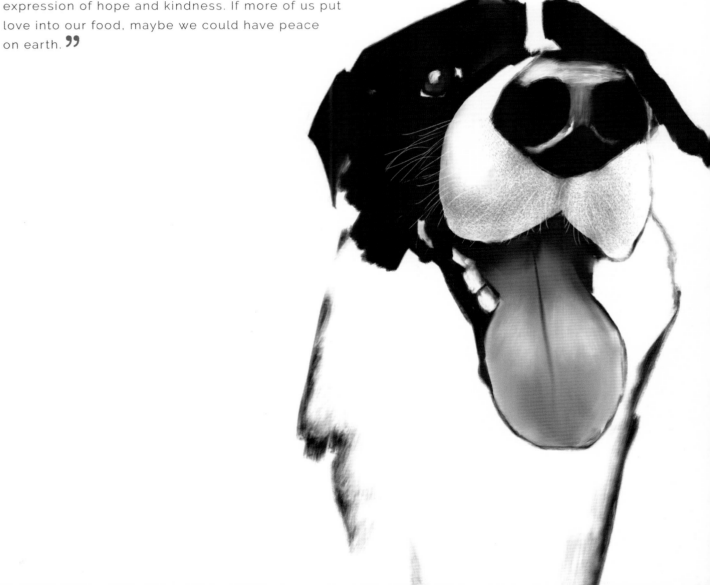

BRENDA

ENJOYS:	A good singalong
SPIRITUAL LEANING:	Yoda seems nice
NOSTALGIC FOR:	The green canvas li-lo
MOST WELL-WORN WARDROBE ITEM:	Birkenstock clogs
MOST EMBARRASSING THING IN THE FRIDGE:	Cheese singles

" I've got a dream. I want to get a bit of acreage in a sleepy little place, somewhere near the sea. I'll build a tiny house from a sea container and make a happy little garden. Natives, mainly, with some marigolds. I'll look after abandoned animals and read the classics, play a bit of Scrabble with friends. They'll be living in the other sea container houses dotted around the place. Close, but not too close. We'll share a veggie patch and grow plenty of chard. Maybe we'll keep a goat for milking. We'll combine our soft plastics, of course. And in the mornings, we'll each raise a small but jaunty flag near our compost bin, so that everyone knows we're still kicking. "

" I drive past her house about twice a day. I change up the times a bit. If her car's there, my heart rate goes up and my palms start to sweat. I don't know what I'm looking for, exactly. Maybe a glimpse of her as she walks past a window. Maybe a glimpse of him. Is this stalking? I don't know. I would never stop the car. I just tootle past looking nonchalant and feeling miserable, but I can't stop myself. I keep going back. It's part of my routine now. "

LIZZIE

SECRET TO SUCCESS:	Never sleep past eleven a.m.
WON'T LEAVE HOME WITHOUT:	Lucky undies
HOUSE RULE:	No smartphones in the toilet
CHEESE OR CHOCOLATE:	Just a cider for me; maybe some artfully scattered almonds
READING:	*Kinfolk* magazine

“ What gets my goat is people
finishing my sentences.
They hardly ever get it right.
Why not just let me do it?
It'd save a lot of time.
Just saying. **”**

"My pet weiro, Kevin, has been missing for two days. I'm in bits. Kevin is epileptic and he's terrified of the dark. He can't sleep without a night-light. It kills me to think about what he's going through. Has he been stolen? Is he hurt? I've taken compassionate leave from work and I've pasted five hundred 'missing' posters around the district. Obviously I'm offering a reward. A big one. Kevin is everything to me. He's not a bird; he's not even a chum. He's my soulmate."

66 I hate the gym, but I love steamed treacle pudding, so I come to Zumba class. I'm not that coordinated, but if I stand directly behind someone who knows what they're doing, I can get at least some of the steps right. I'm still trying to master that tricky pelvic whirlpool manoeuvre, but there are worse dancers than me. You should see this one white chick attempt the booty-shake-fist-pump-salsa-hop. Epic fail every time. The funny thing is, she never smiles about it. 99

GRAHAM

ALWAYS CARRIES:	Cable ties; rarely scissors, though
LONGS FOR:	A torrid affair
STRUGGLES WHEN:	Mercury is in retrograde
ABIDING PHILOSOPHY:	Apologise later
CURRENT GRIPE:	Interrupters

> " I'm worried about the future, to be honest.
> I'm afraid I'm going to turn into that nutbag
> who knits cardigans from plastic bags
> and takes in a lot of stray cats. I need
> to sort out my superannuation. "

" The trouble with Netflix binges is that they really mess with your life. It's not just the lack of greens. It's a bunch of different things. Sleep patterns, sure. All the plot twists are messing with my cortisol levels and I'm short on vitamin D, too. My biorhythms are completely out of whack. But you know the worst thing? I don't find my family very interesting anymore. Their dialogue is slow and sloppy. There's no urgency, hardly any drama. Just foot odour and grunting and loads of laundry. If I had the chance to swap my husband with Jon Snow, I can't be sure what I'd do. "

" I auditioned for NIDA. I didn't get in. When I got the news, I ate a tub of ice-cream and two cabanossi sausages in quick succession. Then I opened my laptop and googled 'dramatic opportunities global'. God bless the internet and its wellspring of ideas. I'm a princess now — I work for Disney On Ice, based out of Beijing. I've played all the leading ladies: Ariel, Cinderella, Pocahontas, Rapunzel. My skating skills have really come along and I get pretty good money, but it's no walk in the park. Sometimes it's insufferable, like the night my boyfriend dumped me right before a show because he'd fallen for a real-life Chinese princess. Oh, the irony. To the audience, my Snow White looked as sweet as pie, but inside I was broken. And bitter. I just wanted to poke Happy's eyes out with a pencil. "

I never chose to be a poster child for my generation. I just nailed this one hell good move on a skateboard and put it up on YouTube. Now I've got sixteen million followers and three sponsorship deals. The free t-shirts are cool, but keeping up with the events schedule is a bit of work. I make heaps of public appearances and I travel a lot. I don't want to complain, but I do find it hard to find time for my first passion, which is making matchstick models in my parents' garage.

HERZEL

ANCESTRY:	A long line of gentleman thieves
GREW UP:	Wearing a cravat most days
TROUBLED BY:	Bitcoin
ADMIRES:	Good joinery
ON THE BUCKET LIST:	The Trans-Siberian Railway

❝ Three a.m. is the worst time.
That's when the demons come. **❞**

ISADORA

PEDIGREE:	Scottish architect father, French ski champion mother
ENJOYS:	Quality time in a hammock
WORKS AT:	Remembering names
PERPLEXED BY:	Cat people
CURRENT OBSESSION:	Can't go past a photo booth

When you live without television, you really miss a lot in conversation. I have no clue who Don Draper is. Or Walter White. Or Keira and Blake and a bunch of others who only have first names. But then again, someone who does know these characters might not know their fungi from their mushrooms, or how to tell when a melon is ripe, or the adorable sound that a coot makes, or what joy there is in finger knitting.

" I see everything in colour. I mean, everything. The days of the week each have a different colour: Saturday is orange; Thursday is dark blue; Tuesday is a surprisingly sunny yellow, for so early in the week. The months have colours, too. So do songs. And family members: my Dad is white, Mum's berry. My best friend is a crazy green — somewhere between chartreuse and pistachio. Man, I love that guy. I love his powder-blue Valiant, too — it's plum. "

" My first job was delivering singing telegrams. Mostly at hens'
and bucks' nights, and other shindigs distinguished by badly
dressed punters drinking cocktails out of buckets. Every
telegram was sung to the same tune — 'That's Amore'.
Listening to that song now, I get flashbacks of flesh and
garters and plumber's cracks and cackling laughter and
testosterone-fuelled roars. I wasn't really cut out for it:
I'm quite shy. I'd often practise my 'I quit' speech on the way
to the gig, but I got fifty bucks a pop from Captain Flamingo's
Singing Telegrams. That was a fair bit back then. Sometimes
I'd get tips, too. I'm told my voice has a lovely cadence.
I'm a family law court judge now. There are worse ways
to launch your career. "

" Camping keeps me from throwing things, so I try to get out bush at least once a month. I do a bit of guerrilla art while I'm out there. Keeps me occupied. I make sculptures out of bits of bark and wood and abandoned wire, the occasional oil rag. I like leaving things in the landscape for others to discover. Last week I made a cougar from a rusty anchor chain, some paperbark and an old leopard-print picnic blanket. I left it crouching on a roadside. That should give the grey nomads something to rubberneck about. "

HARRIET

OCCUPATION:	Horse physio
ADMIRES:	A well put together terrarium
PROUDEST MOMENT:	Uniting an entire peak-hour train carriage in a rousing rendition of 'We Will Rock You'
ASPIRES TO:	Crowd-surf at the symphony, just once
FAVOURITE WORD:	Codswallop

" We saved for a looooong time for our Scandinavian holiday. We planned it for about a year. We wanted to give our three kids memories to last them the rest of their lives, and I'd say we hit most of the stuff on the bucket list. We took a coastal steamer to see the northern lights and built a snowman at the top of the world. We took a dip in some hot springs while giant snowflakes fell around us. We rode snowmobiles and went ice fishing, and ate a shedload of reindeer on pizza. We even went to a ski-through McDonald's. Back on home turf I asked the kids about their favourite moments. Know what topped the list? Riding the travelators at the airport. "

I've been on the speaking circuit for a few years now. Body language is my subject. I do all the power poses in the toilet cubicle beforehand, but the truth is, I've never managed to shake the idea that I don't deserve to be there. It's classic impostor syndrome. Nobody's immune. When I get on stage, I always expect someone to throw shoes.

I know girls are meant to go mad for nice frilly lingerie, but the truth is, I'm wearing blokes' undies. They're so economical, and the seams are super soft. 99

MONTY

PEDIGREE:	Mathematician father, contortionist mother; all five siblings are scientists
BEST KNOWN FOR:	Brilliant fancy-dress repertoire
NEVER MISSES:	The opportunity to dak someone
DAILY HABIT:	A morning ice bath
DREAMS OF:	Getting a knighthood

66 I wish I looked as old as I did the first time I thought I looked old. My advice to the middle aged is to get away from the mirror and just get the hell on with things. Do the poetry performance. Throw the party. Do the silly walk. Go tango dancing. Howl at the moon. Stop to ask perfect strangers about their greatest desires and regrets and dreams. Really suck the marrow out of life, you know? Don't ever flip your phone camera to selfie while you're looking down at it, though. Nothing good ever came from that. 99

" I have eight coffees a day. It used to be twelve, so I've really cut back. I'm aiming for four. Four seems like a number no-one would blink at too much. I don't like to stand out. "

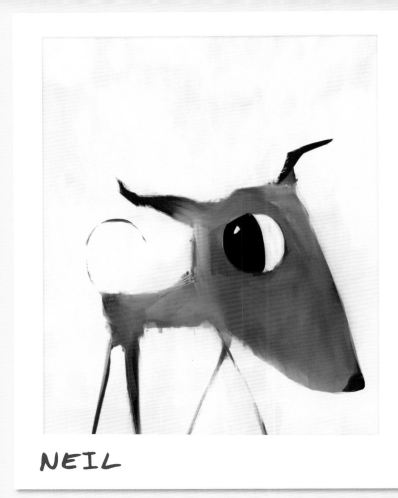

NEIL

LIKES:	Robust discussion
CAN'T ABIDE:	A thoughtlessly brandished exclamation mark
WEAKNESS:	Finger limes
PROUDEST MOMENT:	Scoring an eagle on the thirteenth at St Andrews
REGRETS:	Once packing dried fish with my smalls on a long-haul flight from Norway

" I do worry about the apocalypse. Not so much the apocalypse itself, but life after the apocalypse. Do I even have a single skill to bring to the table? I can't navigate by the stars. I don't know any interesting knots. I can't divine fresh water with a forked stick or light a fire from flint or make a sourdough starter from bellybutton lint. I did do a leadlighting course recently, but I'm not sure there'll be a lot of call for that. "

66 My therapist tells me I have to be kinder to myself. I'm supposed to look in the mirror several times a day and tell myself, 'I love you'. Can you imagine? I'm supposed to totally mean it. 99

" I invent things. My latest project is the nap bar. It's a place where you can go in the middle of a busy day to just lie down and regroup, catch a few zeds. I'm calling it an art installation because I can't face all the red tape from council, but I hope it will become an actual thing. We all need to lie down more. "

"This morning I woke up in somebody's garden, about three blocks from my place. I'm trying to unearth some clues about that. Nothing so far."

JIM

BEST QUALITY:	Straight shooter
ALWAYS CARRIES:	A loaded water pistol
ADMIRES:	Lollipop men and women
DISLIKES:	Ambiguity, sorghum, ill-fitting lids, cliffhanger endings
REALLY WANTS:	A Thermomix

66 I got the giggles at yoga the other day. It was during the chanting at the end. The vibe was pretty Zen as usual but for some reason nobody could hold a tune to save themselves. Maybe it was the waxing moon near the equinox, but whatever it was, no two yogis hit the same note and everyone was loud about it. I had to bury my face in my bolster and think about staples. It was too late though, I couldn't stop. I nearly burst an eardrum trying. Man, I tell you, that om went on. I got the hairy eyeball from a few of the Lululemon crowd, as if I'd farted in church. By the time everyone was muttering namaste with their thumbs on their third eye, I was fully crying. **99**

" We're preppers, me and Nadine. We've been stockpiling bottled water and tinned food in our backyard bunker for a while now. I'm not sure about the exact nature of the catastrophe that's coming, I just know there's probably going to be one. I like to be prepared. Nadine likes decking out interiors. There's a really nice sofa down there, and some on-trend wall macramé. Lots of board games, too. We pooled resources with Graham and Lizzie and bought one of those kickarse vehicles that can drive right over the top of regular cars, in case we have to flee in a hurry. People call us weirdos, but you wait. They'll be tapping on our hatch some day, asking to share our chickpeas. "

" My girlfriend's not good with silences, so she reads things out loud. Street names, shop signage, electronic traffic alerts, signs that say 'Wrong Way Go Back'. At cafes she'll read the entire beverages menu aloud from top to bottom. In some establishments that takes quite a while, especially since turmeric and nut milk got so big. At home, she'll read out the classified ads in the local paper. The irony is, it's a real conversation killer. When she says, 'Handyman. No job too small. Police clearance. Call Wayne', there's really nowhere to go with it. I have nothing to add. Nobody has anything to say about that. "

MIRANDA

FAMILY TRAIT:	Perfect hearing
CAN'T LIVE WITHOUT:	Strappy heels, hair straightener, Berocca
BEWILDERED BY:	The cloud
CURRENT GRIPE:	Living out of a suitcase is pretty tiring
PARTY PIES OR TAPAS:	Just some salad, thanks

"Working in a shop isn't what I thought it would be. I never knew how many criers there would be, for example. Somebody cries in the shop most days, and I'm not even exaggerating. All I have to do is ask someone how their day is going, and the waterworks start. Today I had three before two p.m. I don't encourage them; it's not like I'm a hippie herbal earth mother or anything like that. In fact, if a customer smells like patchouli, I flat out won't serve them. I hate patchouli. That stuff makes me really angry. "

" I get the irrits when customers ask me what I'm studying. I'm not studying anything. I'm a waitress. I'm really, really good at it. They say it's as stressful as being a brain surgeon — without the respect or the support or the money, obviously. I take it seriously. I know how to explain sous-vide without making someone feel stupid. I can carry multiple plates and remember orders in my head and wipe up spills and put out spot fires and talk my co-workers down from a ledge — all while making diners feel completely loved. You know, it's usually the tax auditors who ask me what I'm studying. Next time, I might just ask them when they're going to stop being tax auditors and start doing something useful with their lives. "

" When my wife left me, I was really bad. Not just sad, but angry too. I used to stab the cushions with butter knives. I hit the Temazepam and the rum a bit. Some days I'd lie on the couch and hurl darts at the armchairs. I'm a lot better now. I got new soft furnishings and they're all holding up pretty well. These days when I get down, I'm more inclined to hurl myself into the ocean. There's a lot of healing in there. "

" My job title is Head of Serendipity. When I did my PhD in applied mathematics, I never imagined I'd have that on my business card, but here we are. I work for an app developer. I'm all about creating sweet spots and introducing consumers to stuff they don't even know they want. I don't like to talk about it much. You use terms like denormalised data at a cocktail party, and the light just goes right out of people's eyes. Let's just say I work magic and we won't mention the spreadsheets. **"**

" My perfect Friday night? A bottle of red and a basket of ironing. Pillowcases, of course — everyone knows that's the key to making a bedroom look well put together. But I don't stop at the flat things. I love doing the fiddly shirts as well. And the fitted sheets. It's a bit of a cause of friction between me and my wife, actually. She likes things a bit crumpled. I've tried to win her over on the merits of well-pressed undies. We agree to disagree. "

GERALDINE

GENERAL DISPOSITION:	Cautiously playful
ALWAYS CARRIES:	Gaffer tape
DAILY FOLLY:	Chai latte (in a teapot)
NEVER MISSES:	*Grand Designs*
ABIDING PHILOSOPHY:	Finish what you start — baked goods especially

" There's nothing better than a road trip. I get some of my best ideas in the car, so I always drive with voice memos open on the hands-free. You don't want to be caught short when it occurs to you how you could definitely make your next million from a life-changing new cleaning product, or you've dreamed up a catchy melody that Taylor Swift might like to buy for a handsome fee. I've had a few ideas for romance novels while driving, too. None of my brilliant schemes have come to fruition yet, maybe because I never get around to listening to the voice memos. There always seems to be something more pressing to attend to once I've left the open road and hit the suburbs, just in time for school pick-up. "

66 I'm moving to the country. I don't want
to see traffic lights anymore. 99

“ I'm a bit overwhelmed. There's so much to be good at, isn't there? Everyone on social media seems to manage it. Some days I fantasise about dropping out and going to live in a backwater somewhere, in a fibro shack with an outside loo. No internet. No parent shaming. No filtered photographs. No food porn. No breezily styled interiors. No Pokémon. Actually, I think all the Pokémon are gone now. No Fortnite, that's for sure. And no bloody hashtags. ”

ETHEL

EDUCATION:	Postgraduate anthropology (incomplete)
COLLECTS:	Nautical rope
NEVER MISSES:	A daily shot of wheatgrass
NOSTALGIC FOR:	Dunlop Volleys
FIVE-YEAR PLAN:	Master the croquembouche, finish *Ulysses*, learn ukulele

" Speaking in haiku
gets tiresome for some people,
but I'm fine with it. "

" I'm writing a book on etiquette. Some say it's a dated idea, but I beg to differ. Have you been online lately? It's like the Wild West, and I'm not just talking about trolls here. I'm talking about perfectly reasonable citizens who find themselves part of a WhatsApp chat group with friends. A few things to consider, folks. There's probably no need to say what everyone else just said. Perhaps don't put up a meme that has nothing to do with anything. It's also polite to take a second to gather your thoughts, then send one message rather than ten. I'd suggest exercising a bit of restraint with the prayer hands emoji, too. And don't get me started on the stalker types who read everything in the thread but never contribute anything. Who even are you? "

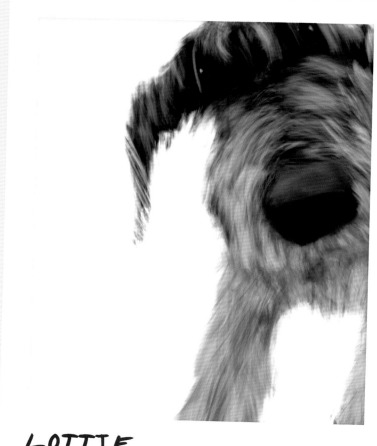

LOTTIE

BEST FEATURE:	Elderflower tattoo, inside wrist
PRIZED POSSESSION:	Vintage collection of *Doctor Who* memorabilia
AMUSED BY:	Latte art
BIG DISAPPOINTMENT:	The avocado slicer
READING:	Sufi poets

<blockquote>
" When I grow up, I'm going to be
an astronaut or a fireman or a fairy.
They have the best costumes. "
</blockquote>

" When I die, I'd like to be planted. You know, in one of those biodegradable pods. Throw a few seeds in there. I hope I'll push up some nice, sturdy flowers in the spring. Don't bother with a fancy headstone. I would like some singing at the funeral, though. Something rousing and ironic. 'Bohemian Rhapsody' could be fun. Feel free to leave part way through if you like. It does go on a bit. **"**

Acknowledgements

This book began life as an exhibition. Thanks, Liz Edmonds, for embracing the idea of having words on the walls at the gorgeous Petrichor Gallery. Lots of visitors to the gallery asked whether it might become a book, and I'm grateful to Fremantle Press for seeing that potential, and making the process such a pleasure.

My evolution in the sometimes bewildering world of digital art has been made smoother by various helping hands. Thanks in particular to Kate Lindsay and Mark Welsh for giving so generously of their time and experience as Hangdog Art found its legs.

Big thanks to the Bugle Club, a bottomless font of good spirits and gentle nudges. And to my family, an artful blend of sounding board, cheer squad and miscellaneous support. Thanks for being such excellent people.

Props finally to Indi for the robust conversation and constructive feedback delivered almost entirely by eyebrow. You're really the best pooch.

About the author

Megan Anderson is an artist and writer based in Fremantle. She paints under the guise of Hangdog Art, and has been a feature writer for *The West Australian* newspaper, editor of *Scoop* magazine, and travel writer for various publications around Australia. She writes stories about humans, and takes direction from a complex golden retriever with a foot fetish.

First published 2019 by
FREMANTLE PRESS

Fremantle Press Inc. trading as Fremantle Press
25 Quarry Street, Fremantle WA 6160
(PO Box 158, North Fremantle WA 6159)
www.fremantlepress.com.au

Printed by Everbest Printing Investment Limited, China
Designed by Amy Moffatt, www.weroamcreative.com

 A catalogue record for this
book is available from the
National Library of Australia

Word of Dog. 9781925816082 (hardback).

Fremantle Press is supported by the State Government
through the Department of Local Government, Sport and
Cultural Industries.

Publication of this title was assisted by the Commonwealth
Government through the Australia Council, its arts funding
and advisory body.

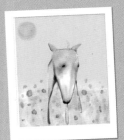